CW00571705

SIMPLE SYMPI

for String Orchestra

(or String Quartet)

BENJAMIN BRITTEN

OXFORD UNIVERSITY PRESS

MUSIC DEPARTMENT · WALTON STREET · OXFORD OX2 6DP

£3.95

Dedicated to Audrey Alston (Mrs. Lincolne Sutton)

SIMPLE SYMPHONY

I
BOISTEROUS BOURRÉE

BENJAMIN BRITTEN

⊕ From Suite No. I (for piano)- 1926

Copyright, 1935, by the Oxford University Press, London. Renewed in U.S.A. 1963. Printed in Great Britain
OXFORD UNIVERSITY PRESS, MUSIC DEPARTMENT, WALTON STREET, OXFORD OX2 6DP
Photocopying this copyright material is **ILLEGAL**

3

Song - 1923

4

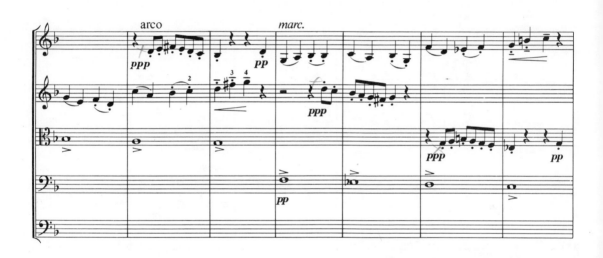

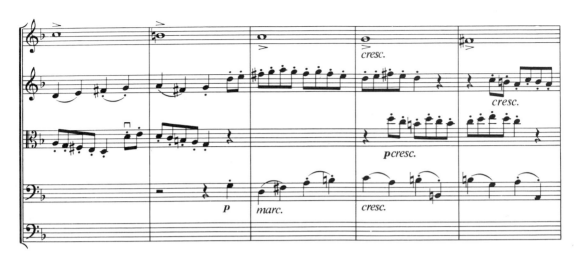

* If there is only one Cello, the first part is to be taken

8

Allargando

⑧ **Animato**

⑨ Tempo Iᵐᵒ

II
PLAYFUL PIZZICATO

✛ Scherzo (piano) 1924

† The second set of numbers is to be read when repeating the first section

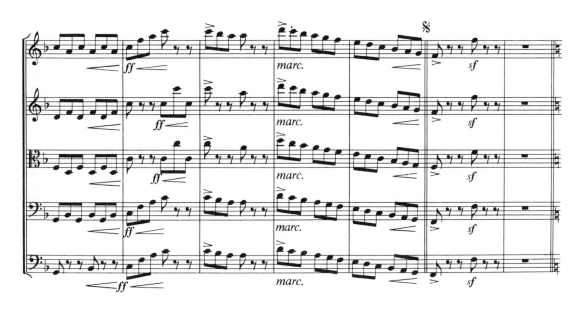

14

TRIO

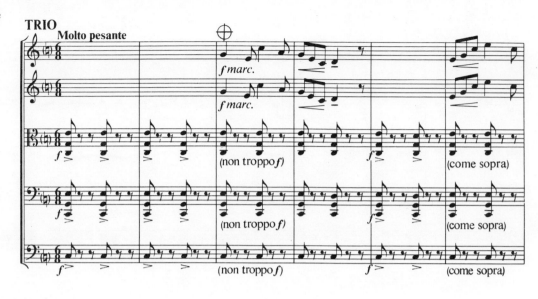

⊕ Song - 1924

D.C. subito sin' al 𝄌 e poi la Coda

CODA

III
SENTIMENTAL SARABAND

⊕ From Suite No. 3 (for piano) - 1925

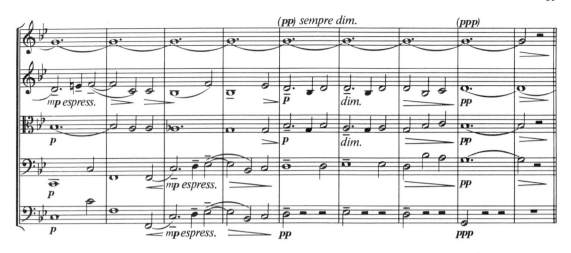

Poco più tranquillo

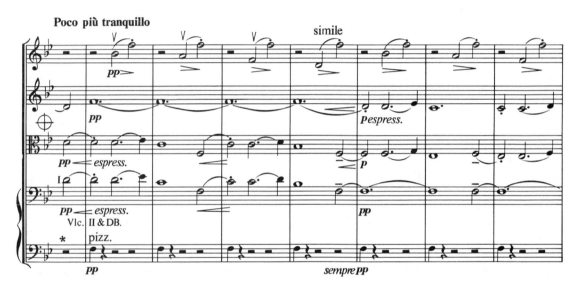

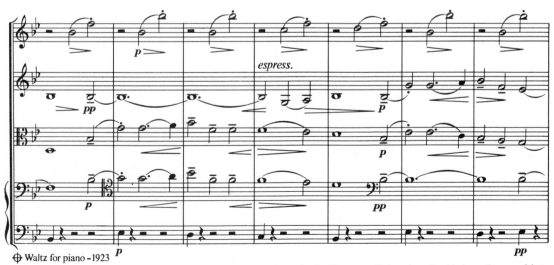

⊕ Waltz for piano - 1923

* If there is only one Cello, but also a Double-bass, the Cello is to take the first part; if there is no Double-bass, the second is to be taken (with alterations in small type) as far as ④ – after that the first.

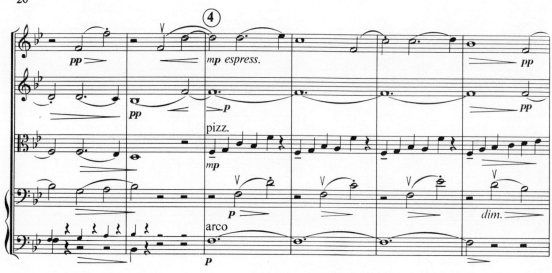

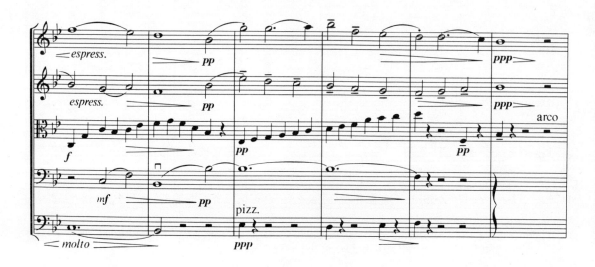

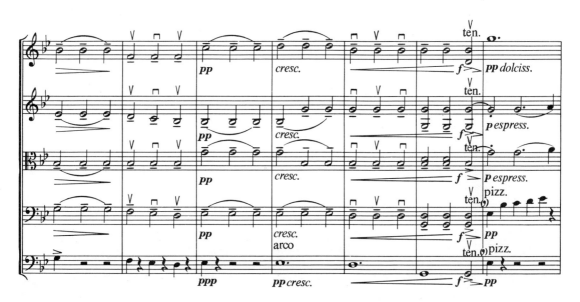

IV
FROLICSOME FINALE

From piano Sonata No. 9 - 1926

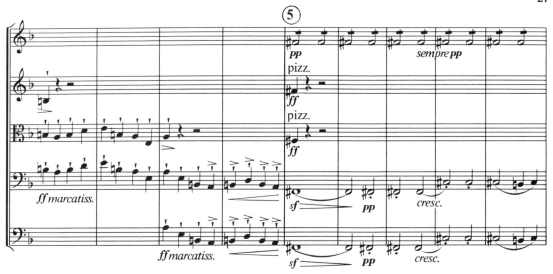

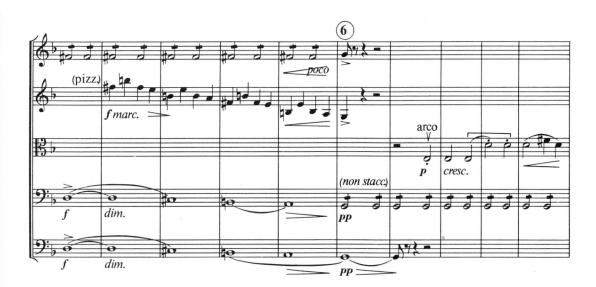

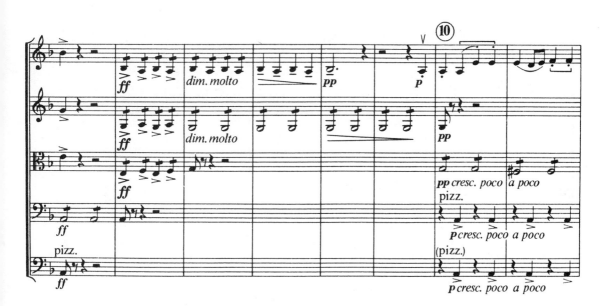

8va ad libitum

* Topnotes optional (shown by
brackets)

Reproduced and printed by
Halstan & Co. Ltd., Amersham, Bucks., England

[Dec. 23, 1933 - Feb. 10, 1934]

OXFORD UNIVERSITY PRESS